Arctic Adventures Coloring Book

Thank you for choosing Ava Browne Coloring Books.
We strive to publish unique coloring books for all ages.

Visit us at www.Avabrowne.com and sign up to our free newsletter. All new subscribers receive a FREE 10 Page PDF Coloring Book! Join our active and growing Facebook Community at www.facebook.com/groups/avabrownecoloring All group members receive a FREE 20 Page PDF Coloring Book!

This coloring book contains double images, meaning you get to try different colors and shading for every page!!

If you found this coloring book enjoyable, please leave us a review. Reviews help drive sales which allows us to make more coloring books.

This book also includes a free digital copy that you can print out at home. For instructions and your access code, please go to the last page.

If you have any questions please contact us at:
avabrownebooks@gmail.com

Thank you and happy coloring!

COLOR TEST PAGE

COLOR TEST PAGE

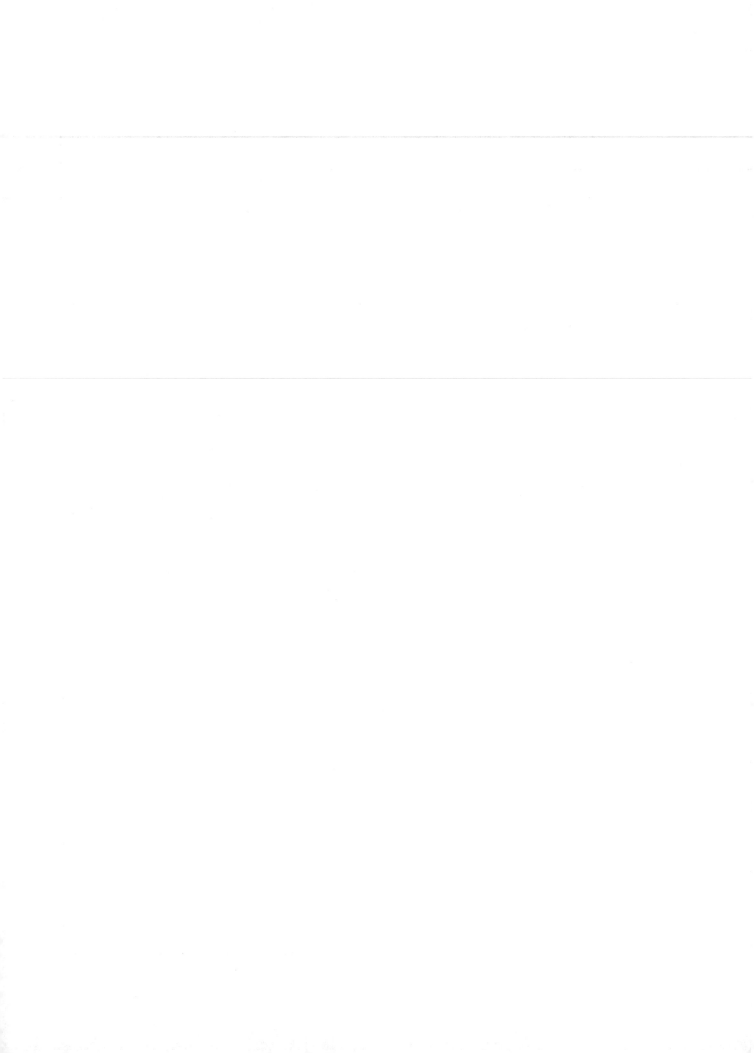

DUPLICATE PAGES START HERE

WE PROVIDE DOUBLE PAGES SO CAN COLOR YOUR FAVORITE IMAGES TWICE USING DIFFERENT TECHNIQUES, SHARE WITH A FRIEND, OR REDO BECAUSE OF A MISTAKE.

DON'T FORGET TO VISIT AVABROWNE.COM TO DOWNLOAD YOUR FREE DIGITAL EDITION WHICH CAN BE PRINTED AND COLORED AS MANY TIMES AS YOU LIKE!

THE DOWNLOAD LINK AND PASSWORD ARE LOCATED ON THE LAST PAGE OF THIS BOOK.

Please visit
https://avabrowne.com/arctic-adventures-download/
to download your free digital copy.
Enter the password
72gwkpv
to access the file.(All Lowercase)

Made in United States
Orlando, FL
16 December 2024

55528708R00070